Collins

Collins
Spanish
Idioms

HarperCollins Publishers
Westerhill Road
Bishopbriggs
Glasgow
G64 2QT
Great Britain

First Edition 2010

Reprint 10 9 8 7 6 5 4 3 2 1 0

© HarperCollins Publishers 2010

Collins® is a registered trademark of
HarperCollins Publishers Limited

www.collinslanguage.com

A catalogue record for this book is
available from the British Library

ISBN 978-0-00-733736-1

Designed and typeset by Thomas Callan

Printed in Great Britain by
Clays Ltd, St Ives plc

Acknowledgements
We would like to thank those authors
and publishers who kindly gave
permission for copyright material
to be used in the Collins Word Web.
We would also like to thank Times
Newspapers Ltd for providing valuable
data.

PUBLISHING DIRECTOR
Rob Scriven

MANAGING EDITOR
Gaëlle Amiot-Cadey

PROJECT MANAGEMENT
Susie Beattie
Jeremy Butterfield
Ben Harris

CONTRIBUTORS
José Antonio Gálvez Castiella
Sinda López Fuentes
Teresa Álvarez García

ILLUSTRATION AND IMAGE RESEARCH
Q2AMedia

William Collins' dream of knowledge for all began with the publication of his first book in 1819. A self-educated mill worker, he not only enriched millions of lives, but also founded a flourishing publishing house. Today, staying true to this spirit, Collins books are packed with inspiration, innovation, and practical expertise. They place you at the centre of a world of possibility and give you exactly what you need to explore it.

Language is the key to this exploration, and at the heart of Collins Dictionaries is language as it is really used. New words, phrases, and meanings spring up every day, and all of them are captured and analysed by the Collins Word Web. Constantly updated, and with over 2.5 billion entries, this living language resource is unique to our dictionaries. Words are tools for life. And a Collins Dictionary makes them work for you.

Collins. Do more.

Introduction

What is it?

Collins Easy Learning Spanish Idioms is an invaluable resource for learners
of Spanish who want to be able to communicate more naturally. It
will enable you to start to include colourful idiomatic phrases and
expressions in both your writing and conversation, increasing your
confidence and effectiveness. It can be used to develop your language
skills, whether you are studying Spanish at school or university, at home
or at an evening class.

Why do you need it?

Developing expertise in writing, speaking and understanding a foreign
language means being able to pull together and build on a number of
different aspects – vocabulary, grammar, pronunciation, and so on. An
important element of increased proficiency in communication is the use
of idioms and figurative expressions which will add colour and variety
to your writing and conversation as well as enabling you to sound more
natural and confident. Idioms are phrases whose meaning may not be
obvious from the words they contain. For example, a common English
idiom is 'Add fuel to the fire'. If somebody adds fuel to the fire, they
make a bad situation worse.

How is it structured?

Collins Easy Learning Spanish Idioms has been carefully designed to provide
a rich and easy-to-use resource for extending your language skills. It

contains 250 phrases and expressions, all of which have been selected because they are commonly used by Spanish speakers today. These idioms are then grouped under 25 themes. Each of these themes covers an area of everyday life or experience, such as 'Health, happiness, pleasure and enjoyment', 'Madness, foolishness and stupidity', and 'Directness, decisiveness and expressing opinions'.

For maximum clarity, each Spanish idiom is followed by a word-for-word English translation as well as the equivalent idiomatic expression(s) that you would use in English. In many cases, a short background note is included if some explanation or additional information about Spanish language or culture is required. Then, in order to illustrate the use of the idiom in a natural context, a sentence or two of Spanish is provided. Again, this is translated into idiomatic English. For example:

estar como unas castañuelas

> *"to be like a pair of castanets"*
> = to be as happy as Larry
> = to be as happy as a clam

What could be more typically Spanish than to use the merry, energizing sound of castanets to describe happiness?

Está como unas castañuelas porque ha aprobado el examen.
He's as happy as Larry because he's passed the exam.

Why choose Collins Easy Learning Spanish Idioms?

- **easy to use**: 250 colourful idiomatic expressions arranged in 25 themes to do with daily life and common experience
- **easy to read**: a clear, modern layout which allows you to find the information you want quickly and easily
- **easy to understand**: written in an accessible style with the language you will hear from Spanish speakers today

The Collins Easy Learning range

The Collins Easy Learning Spanish Idioms is the latest addition to the bestselling Collins Easy Learning range, which includes the highly acclaimed Collins Easy Learning Spanish Dictionary. Collins Easy Learning Spanish Grammar and Collins Easy Learning Spanish Verbs support you with all your grammatical needs, while the Collins Easy Learning Spanish Words and Collins Easy Learning Spanish Conversation allow you to learn and practise your Spanish vocabulary and communication skills. The Collins Easy Learning series is the ideal language reference range to help you learn Spanish.

Contents

Health, happiness, pleasure and enjoyment

Unhappiness, sickness, grief and disappointment

Achievement, success, failure and misfortune

Contents

Hope, dreams, fear and anxiety

Anger, annoyance, threats and violence

Truth, honesty, lying and deceit

Love, affection, marriage and friendship

Contents

Mistakes, shame and embarrassment

Knowledge, intelligence, ignorance and understanding

Looks, appearance, beauty and vanity

Contents

Madness, foolishness and stupidity

Relationships, similarities and differences

Problems, difficulties, the possible and the impossible

Contents

Orders, obedience, control and equality

Work, achievement, effort and ambition

Change, continuity, risk and opportunity

Motion, travel, leaving and parting

Chance, surprise and the unexpected

Contents

Eating, drinking, drunkenness and excess

Directness, decisiveness and expressing opinions

Money, debt, wealth and poverty

Language, speech, silence and conversation

Contents

Youth, experience, age and death

Easy Learning Spanish Idioms

Health, happiness, pleasure and enjoyment

estar como unas castañuelas

> *"to be like a pair of castanets"*
> = to be as happy as Larry
> = to be as happy as a clam

What could be more typically Spanish than to use the merry, energizing sound of castanets to describe happiness?

Está como unas castañuelas porque ha aprobado el examen.
He's as happy as Larry because he's passed the exam.

estar más sano que una pera

"to be healthier than a pear"
= to be as fit as a fiddle

Pears come into a couple of other colourful phrases you can find in this book.

Tiene ochenta años pero está más sano que una pera.
He's eighty, but he's as fit as a fiddle.

disfrutar como un enano

"to enjoy yourself like a dwarf"
= to have a brilliant time

Dwarves at the Spanish court kept the royal children company, and led a privileged life, as can be seen in Spanish paintings of the 17th century, for instance by Velázquez.

José disfrutó como un enano en la playa.
José had a brilliant time at the beach.

tener cara de pascua

"to have an Easter face"
= to be grinning from ear to ear

This phrase comes from the fact that Easter is a time of religious rejoicing.

¡Qué suerte tuvo! No me sorprendió que tuviera cara de pascua.
He was really lucky. I'm not surprised he was grinning from ear to ear.

sobre gustos no hay nada escrito

"about taste there's nothing written down"
= there's no accounting for taste

You use this to suggest that something somebody else enjoys isn't really your cup of tea. It must be very old, as it is similar to a classic Latin phrase.

Si a ti te encantó, me parece perfecto, sobre gustos no hay nada escrito.
If you loved it, that's fine. There's no accounting for taste.

hasta las tantas

"until the so many (hours)"
= till all hours

If you were out really late enjoying yourself, you could use this phrase to tell somebody just how late.

Estuvimos charlando hasta las tantas.
We were chatting away till all hours.

ser más fuerte que un roble

"to be stronger than an oak tree"
= to be as strong as an ox

If you're healthy and strong, you can also be described as **más fuerte que un toro** (*stronger than a bull*).

Es más fuerte que un roble. Consiguió mover el armario sin pestañear.
He's as strong as an ox. He managed to move the wardrobe without batting an eyelid.

Unhappiness, sickness, grief and disappointment

aburrirse como una ostra

"to be as bored as an oyster"
= to be bored rigid
= to be bored to death

Though oysters are a delicacy in Spain, they don't have a very exciting life.

Me aburro como una ostra, vámonos.
I'm bored rigid, let's go.

llevar a alguien por la calle de la amargura

"to lead somebody down misery street"
= to make somebody's life a misery

Desde que perdió el trabajo, su marido la lleva por la calle de la amargura.
Ever since he lost his job, her husband has been making her life a misery.

estar hasta las narices de algo/alguien

"to be up to the nostrils with something/somebody"
= to be fed up to the back teeth with something/
somebody

Narices (*nostrils*) is the plural of nariz (*nose*). Another way of saying you're fed up is **estar hasta la coronilla** (*to be up to the crown of your head*).

Estoy hasta las narices de sus impertinencias.
I'm fed up to the back teeth with his cheek.

tragar sapos

"to swallow toads"

= to go through hell

If you have to put up with something you don't like, swallowing toads conveys the idea nicely. Even more grisly is **tragar sapos y culebras** (*to swallow toads and snakes*).

Tuvo que tragar sapos para conseguir salvar su matrimonio.
He had to go through hell to save his marriage.

no estar para fiestas

> *"not to be in the mood for parties"*
> = to be in no mood for fun and games

Mejor salimos otro día, hoy no estoy para fiestas.
It's best if we go out another day, I'm in no mood for fun and games.

no tiene ni padre ni madre ni perrito que le ladre

> *"he/she doesn't have a father or a mother or a little dog to bark for him/her"*
> = he/she is all alone in the world

Like many colourful Spanish phrases, this one has a rhyme in it.

Se ha quedado viudo y no tiene ni padre ni madre ni perrito que le ladre.
He's been widowed and he's all alone in the world.

llorar como una magdalena

"to cry like a Mary Magdalene"
= to cry your eyes out
= to cry your heart out

This phrase comes from the grief of Mary Magdalene at the Crucifixion.

Todos en el velatorio lloraban como una magdalena.
Everyone at the wake was crying their eyes out.

no estar muy católico

"not to be feeling very Catholic"
= to be feeling a bit under the weather

Hoy no estoy muy católico, me voy a acostar un rato.
I'm feeling a bit under the weather today. I think I'll have a lie down.

se le cayó el alma a los pies

"his soul sank to his feet"
= his heart sank

Other Spanish phrases you'll see in this book refer to **el alma** where English talks about your *heart*. In this one, it could hardly sink any further.

Cuando se enteró de la noticia, se le cayó el alma a los pies.
When he heard the news, his heart sank.

más se perdió en Cuba

"more was lost in Cuba"

= it's not the end of the world

= worse things happen at sea

Cuba was the last Spanish colony, and its loss in 1898 was felt to be a catastrophe. If somebody has suffered a setback, you use this phrase to put it in perspective.

¡Tranquilízate! No es una buena noticia, pero más se perdió en Cuba.

Calm down! It may not be good news, but it's not the end of the world.

Achievement, success, failure and misfortune

las vacas gordas

"the fat cows"
= boom years

● Though this seems like a farming image, it may well come from the Bible, from Genesis.

Se enriqueció durante las vacas gordas.
He got rich during the boom years.

poner una pica en Flandes

"to put a pike in Flanders"
= to pull something off

Spain fought campaigns in Flanders in the seventeenth century, but it was hard to get men to volunteer to fight there – to carry pikes.

Ahora que leyó nuestra propuesta, ya hemos puesto una pica en Flandes.
Now that he's read our proposal, I think we've basically pulled it off.

ir viento en popa

"to go wind in the stern"
= to be going splendidly

The image here comes from sailing. If the wind is coming from the stern of the boat, it fills the sails and the boat moves easily.

El proyecto va viento en popa.
The project is going splendidly.

quedar en humo de paja

"to end up as smoke from straw"
= to come to nothing

Esperemos que el acuerdo no quede en humo de paja.
Let's hope that the agreement doesn't come to nothing.

sacar agua de las piedras

"to get water out of stones"
= to work miracles

Es una persona increíble, consigue sacar agua de las piedras.
He's incredible. He manages to work miracles.

no caerá esa breva

> *"that early fig won't drop"*
> = chance would be a fine thing

● The idea is that the fig isn't ripe enough to fall from the tree.

–**A lo mejor se acuerda de ti y te invita.**
–**No caerá esa breva.**
"Perhaps he'll remember you and invite you."
"Chance would be a fine thing!"

tener mala pata

> *"to have a bad leg"*
> = to be unlucky

● Pata usually refers to an animal's leg but is also an informal word for a person's leg.

¡Qué mala pata tengo! He vuelto a perder el tren.
I'm so unlucky! I've missed the train again.

ir sobre ruedas

"to go on wheels"
= to go smoothly

The idea here is that if something is on wheels, it runs
smoothly.

No te preocupes, que todo va sobre ruedas.
Don't worry, everything's going smoothly.

otro gallo te cantaría

"another cockerel would crow for you"
= it would have been a different story

The reference here is religious: to the cock that crowed when Saint Peter denied that he knew Jesus.

Si hubiera estudiado más, otro gallo me cantaría.
If I'd studied harder, it would have been a different story.

llueve sobre mojado

"it rains on what's already wet"
= it never rains but it pours

Primero la crisis mundial y ahora la gripe A: llueve sobre mojado.
First the credit crunch, and now swine flu: it never rains but it pours.

tirarse de las barbas

"to tear your beard out"
= to be tearing your hair out

Beards loom large in Spanish culture, and this is one example of the many phrases in which they figure.

Se tiraba de las barbas por no haberse dado cuenta del error.
He was tearing his hair out because he hadn't noticed the mistake.

para más inri

"for more inri"
= to cap it all
= to make matters worse

This is another religious reference. The Latin sign **INRI** – standing for Jesus of Nazareth, King of the Jews – was placed on the cross.

Y, para más inri, ni siquiera se despidió.
And, to cap it all, he didn't even say goodbye.

éramos pocos y parió la abuela

"there were only a few of us and grandma had a baby"
= just when we thought things couldn't get any worse
= that's all we needed
= that's just what we needed

If you picture a family struggling to make ends meet, and then grandma has a baby too, it's hard to imagine things getting any worse!

Y ahora llega mi primo. ¡Éramos pocos y parió la abuela!
And now here comes my cousin. That's all we needed!

Hope, dreams, fear and anxiety

hacer las cuentas de la lechera

"to do the milkmaid's sums"

= to count your chickens before they're hatched

In a classic Spanish story, a milkmaid on her way to market daydreams about what she's going to do with her earnings. When she drops her milk, her dream is shattered.

Tienes que ser más realista. Estás haciendo las cuentas de la lechera.

You need to be more realistic. You're counting your chickens before they're hatched.

esperar algo como agua de mayo

> *"to hope for something like rain in May"*
> = to eagerly await something

In a dry country like Spain, rain in May is something that farmers long for to help their crops.

Esperan el anuncio de las ayudas públicas como agua de mayo.
They're eagerly awaiting the government's announcement of help.

mi sueño dorado

> *"my golden dream"*
> = my dream

Something you really want in Spanish isn't merely a dream, it's a golden dream.

El mundial es el sueño dorado de muchos futbolistas.
The World Cup is many footballers' dream.

tener el alma en un hilo

"to have your soul on a string"
= to be worried sick

Here's another phrase which uses **el alma** where English talks about your *heart*.

Los padres del niño extraviado tienen el alma en un hilo.
The missing child's parents are worried sick.

no es tan fiero el león como lo pintan

"the lion is not as fierce as he is painted"
= his bark is worse than his bite

You can also say **perro que ladra, poco muerde** (*a dog that barks doesn't bite much*).

Puedes hablar con él, no es tan fiero el león como lo pintan.
You can speak to him: his bark is worse than his bite.

liarse la manta a la cabeza

"to tie your cape over your head"
= to take the plunge

You may be afraid, but if you tie your cape round your head you can't see the dangers that lie in wait.

Un buen día, se lió la manta a la cabeza y se fue a vivir a Marruecos.
One fine day, he took the plunge and went off to live in Morocco.

hacer de tripas corazón

"to make a heart out of your guts"
= to pluck up the courage

Hice de tripas corazón y le pedí perdón.
I plucked up the courage and apologized to her.

temblar como un flan

> *"to shake like a crème caramel"*
> = to shake like a jelly
> = to shake like a leaf

🔵 **Flan** (*crème caramel*) is a staple dessert in the Hispanic world, and can wobble just as much as jelly.

Cuando comenzó la entrevista, temblaba como un flan.
At the start of the interview, I was shaking like a leaf.

Anger, annoyance, threats and violence

estar hecho un ají

"to be a chilli"

= to be hopping mad

This expression is more commonly used in Latin America.

Cuando me llamó, estaba hecho un ají.
When he called me, he was hopping mad.

estar hecho un basilisco

> *"to be a basilisk"*
> = to be hopping mad

● A basilisk is a mythical creature, hatched by a snake from a cock's egg, a mere look from which was fatal. How angry is that?

Cuando entré en clase, el profesor estaba hecho un basilisco.
When I went into class, the teacher was hopping mad.

¿qué mosca le habrá picado?

> *"which fly can have bitten him?"*
> = what's got into him?
> = who rattled his cage?

No me ha saludado, ¿qué mosca le habrá picado?
He didn't say hello. I wonder what's got into him?

perder los estribos

"to lose your stirrups"
= to lose your temper
= to fly off the handle

● The idea here is that your temper is like a horse you lose control of.

Es una persona muy tranquila que nunca pierde los estribos.
He's a very calm person who never flies off the handle.

mandar a alguien a freír espárragos

"to tell somebody to go and fry asparagus"
= to tell somebody to get lost

Me molestó tanto que acabé mandándola a freír espárragos.
She annoyed me so much that in the end I told her to get lost.

hacerse mala sangre

"to make yourself bad blood"
= to upset yourself
= to get hot under the collar

You mostly use this phrase in the negative, when telling somebody to calm down.

No te hagas mala sangre, no vale la pena.
Don't upset yourself, it's not worth it.

soltar ajos y cebollas

"to come out with garlics and onions"

= to swear

= to let rip

This expression is more commonly used in Latin America.

Cuando veo cosas así, me entran ganas de soltar ajos y cebollas.
Seeing things like that makes me want to let rip.

tener cara de acelga

> *"to have a face like Swiss chard"*
> = to have a face a mile long

How can a person who is annoyed look like a leaf vegetable? Swiss chard has a long, slender leaf, hence the image of a furious, long face.

¿Por qué tienes esa cara de acelga?
Why have you got a face a mile long?

Truth, honesty, lying and deceit

dar a alguien gato por liebre

"to give somebody cat instead of hare"
= to sell somebody a pig in a poke
= to pull a fast one on somebody

Dishonest butchers used to sell cat meat as highly prized hare meat, especially after the Spanish Civil War, when food was scarce.

Tengo bastante experiencia, no me vas a dar gato por liebre.
I've got quite a lot of experience – you're not going to pull a fast one on me.

las mentiras tienen patas cortas

"lies have short legs"
= truth will out

If you visualize lies as terriers with stumpy little legs, you'll quickly understand that they won't get very far.

Hoy puede que consiga engañar a alguien, pero las mentiras tienen patas cortas.
He might be able to get away with it today, but truth will out.

cuéntaselo a tu abuela

"tell that to your grandmother"
= pull the other one

If you don't believe what somebody is saying, you can suggest they tell the same story to their gran, who will, of course, believe them! You'd need to know somebody very well to use this phrase.

¿El autobús no pasó? ¡Cuéntaselo a tu abuela!
The bus didn't come? Pull the other one!

tomar algo con pinzas

"to take something with tongs"
= to take something with a pinch of salt

Just as you'd pick up something hot like a lump of coal with tongs, so you need to be very careful with what some people tell you.

Yo esa afirmación la tomaría con pinzas.
I would take that statement with a pinch of salt.

dale el pie y te tomará la mano

"give him your foot and he'll take your hand"
= give him an inch and he'll take a mile

Ten mucho cuidado con él, dale el pie y te tomará la mano.
Be very careful with him: give him an inch and he'll take a mile.

andar con mucho ojo

"to go with a lot of eye"
= to keep your wits about you
= to be very careful

Apart from its basic meaning of *eye*, **ojo** is used to mean *be careful*.

Anda con mucho ojo que el centro de la ciudad es bastante peligroso.
Keep your wits about you because the centre of town is rather dangerous.

untar la mano de alguien

"to grease somebody's hand"
= to grease somebody's palm

Se libró de la multa untando la mano del policía.
He got out of paying by greasing the policeman's palm.

no es trigo limpio

"he isn't clean wheat"
= he isn't to be trusted

En esa oficina nadie es trigo limpio.
No one can be trusted in that office.

decir digo donde dije Diego

"to say 'digo' where I said 'Diego'"
= to go back on your word

A tongue-twister and a pun at the same time.

Nos prometió el viaje y ahora, donde dije digo, digo Diego.
He promised us the trip and now he's going back on his word.

Love, affection, marriage and friendship

mi media naranja

"my half orange"
= my other half

● You can apply this expression to your other half, or to the person of your dreams that you're searching for.

¿Puedo llevar a la fiesta a mi media naranja?
Can I bring my other half to the party?

beber los aires por alguien

"to drink the breezes for somebody"
= to be madly in love with somebody

You can also use the expression **beber los vientos por alguien** (*to drink the winds for somebody*).

Bebe los aires por una chica de su clase.
He's madly in love with a girl in his class.

pelar la pava

"to peel the turkey"
= to whisper sweet nothings
= to smooch

The story goes that a maid was skinning a turkey by a window and spent ages chatting to her boyfriend there. When her mistress called, she replied: **Es que aún estoy pelando la pava** (*I'm still skinning the turkey*).

Se pasaron la tarde pelando la pava.
They spent the evening smooching.

ser el ojo derecho de alguien

"to be somebody's right eye"
= to be the apple of somebody's eye

Why the right eye? Because the right-hand side is traditionally good and positive, as opposed to the left, which is bad or sinister.

Sara es el ojo derecho de la profesora.
Sara is the apple of the teacher's eye.

poner los cuernos a alguien

"to put horns on somebody"
= to cheat on somebody

Though no longer a living image in English, horns are the traditional symbol of the cheated husband, often mentioned, for instance, in Shakespeare.

Le pone los cuernos a su mujer.
He's cheating on his wife.

ser un pedazo de pan

"to be a piece of bread"
= to be a real sweetie

Also common, and slightly more informal, is **ser un cacho de pan.**

Mi hermana es un pedazo de pan.
My sister is a real sweetie.

son como chanchos

"they're like pigs"
= they're as thick as thieves

Se conocieron hace poco y ya son como chanchos.
They only met recently and already they're as thick as thieves.

estar a partir un piñón

> *"to be close enough to split a pine nut"*
> = to be bosom buddies

Pine nuts, occasionally used in Hispanic cooking, are even smaller than peanuts. You'd have to be really good friends to share one.

Mi hermana y Julia están a partir un piñón.
My sister and Julia are bosom buddies.

hacer buenas migas

> *"to make good crumbs"*
> = to hit it off

The story behind this very old phrase is this: shepherds made a simple meal of fat and **migas** (*crumbs*). If the ingredients are good they bind well together, just like good friends.

Los niños hicieron buenas migas rápidamente.
The children hit it off very quickly.

Argument, conflict, help
and cooperation

no apearse del burro

"not to get down from your donkey"
= to refuse to back down

Hemos intentado dialogar con ella pero no se apea del burro.
We've tried to talk to her, but she refuses to back down.

se armó la de San Quintín

> *"what happened at San Quintín broke out"*
> = there was an almighty rumpus
> = all hell broke loose

This venerable phrase refers to the Spanish taking the
French town of Saint Quentin in a bloody battle, in 1557.
It was to commemorate this great victory that Philip II
ordered the famous palace **El Escorial** to be built.

Cuando el profesor salió de la clase, se armó la de San Quintín.
When the teacher left the classroom, all hell broke loose.

llevar el agua a su molino

> *"to lead the water to your own mill"*
> = to turn things to your own advantage

Water being historically a scarce resource in parts of Spain,
there were often disputes over who used it, and crafty
millers would divert it.

Es normal que cada uno quiera llevar el agua a su molino.
It's normal for everyone to want to turn things to their own
advantage.

arrimar el ascua a su sardina

"to put the coals close to your own sardine"
= to look after number one

● Obviously, if several people are barbecuing sardines and you put yours nearest the coals, it will cook first. Very selfish.

Es de los que siempre intenta arrimar el ascua a su sardina.
He's one of those people who always try to look after number one.

echar pelillos a la mar

"to throw little hairs into the sea"
= to bury the hatchet

● 'But I thought **el mar** was masculine', I hear you say. You are absolutely right. But in some phrases it becomes the feminine **la mar**, as here.

Pues nos damos un abrazo y echamos pelillos a la mar.
Well let's have a hug and bury the hatchet.

nunca llueve a gusto de todos

> *"it never rains to everyone's taste"*
> = you can never please everybody

Como nunca llueve a gusto de todos, hubo unos pocos que protestaron por la decisión.
As you can never please everybody, there were a few people who complained about the decision.

decir amén a todo

> *"to say amen to everything"*
> = to say yes to everything
> = to be a yes man

Aunque no estés de acuerdo, tú di amén a todo.
Even if you don't agree, just say yes to everything.

tener a alguien entre ojos

"to have somebody between your eyes"
= to have it in for somebody

 A related phrase with the same meaning is **tener a alguien entre ceja y ceja** (*to have somebody between eyebrow and eyebrow*).

Tengo a Carlos entre ojos.
I've got it in for Carlos.

romper una lanza a favor de alguien

"to break a lance for somebody"

= to stick your neck out for somebody

Quería romper una lanza a favor del criticado presidente.
I wanted to stick my neck out for the president, who had been criticized.

Telling off, praise, critics and criticism

poner a alguien por las nubes

"to put somebody in the clouds"
= to praise somebody to the skies

The English and Spanish phrases are quite similar, but the Spanish is more specific.

En la reseña ponen al director por las nubes.
In the review, the director is praised to the skies.

leer la cartilla a alguien

"to read the primer to somebody"
= to read somebody the riot act
= to take somebody to task

In olden days, **cartillas** (*primers*) were very simple books with the ABC from which children learnt to read and write. If you read it out to somebody, you're making sure they remember it.

Si no apruebo todas, mis padres me van a leer la cartilla.
If I don't pass all my subjects, my parents are going to read me the riot act.

poner a alguien como un trapo

"to leave somebody like a rag"
= to tear somebody to shreds

Cuando descubrió lo que había hecho, el profesor me puso como un trapo.
When he found out what I'd done, the teacher really tore me to shreds.

ser canela fina

"to be fine cinnamon"
= to be quality
= to be real class

El reparto de esa película es canela fina.
The cast of that film is real class.

que da gloria

"that gives glory"
= wonderfully

Cocina que da gloria.
She's a wonderful cook.

lo dijo de labios para fuera

"he said it from the lips outwards"
= he didn't really mean it

● You use this very physical phrase to criticize somebody by suggesting that they are insincere.

Afirmó que estaba encantado pero sé que lo dijo de labios para fuera.
He said he was delighted, but I know he didn't really mean it.

no tener nombre

"not to have a name"
= to be unspeakable
= to be despicable

Lo que hicieron contigo no tiene nombre.
What they did to you is despicable.

hablar pestes de alguien

"to talk plagues about somebody"
= to badmouth somebody
= to slag somebody off

Siempre que no está delante, habla pestes de su suegra.
Whenever she's not around, he slags his mother-in-law off.

regalar el oído a alguien

"to regale somebody's ears"
= to flatter somebody

Elógiale, le encanta que le regalen el oído.
Praise him, he loves to be flattered.

de mala muerte

"of a bad death"
= ghastly
= horrible

Tuvimos que pasar la noche en un hotel de mala muerte.
We had to spend the night in a ghastly hotel.

Mistakes, shame and embarrassment

ser como guitarra en un entierro

"to be like a guitar at a funeral"
= to be completely out of place
= to stick out like a sore thumb

Con esa ropa eres como una guitarra en un entierro.
With those clothes on, you're completely out of place.

meter la pata

"to put your leg"
= to put your foot in it

Pata is an informal word for *leg*. You can also use another slang word for *leg* in the expression **meter la gamba**.

Creo que he metido la pata.
I think I've put my foot in it.

como un tomate

"as red as a tomato"
= as red as a beetroot

You can also say **rojo como un tomate**.

Al subir al escenario se puso como un tomate.
When he got up on stage he turned as red as a beetroot.

ponerse como un ají

"to look like a chilli"
= to go bright red

Cuando la chica le sonrió, se puso como un ají.
When the girl smiled at him he went bright red.

fulminar a alguien con la mirada

"to strike somebody with lightning with a look"
= to look daggers at somebody

This is the kind of withering look you give somebody who has just done or said something very indiscreet.

Le interrumpí sin querer y me fulminó con la mirada.
I interrupted him without meaning to and he looked daggers at me.

quedar a la altura del betún

"to be left at the height of shoe polish"
= to make yourself look really bad

If you've done something embarrassing, it would be hard to feel much lower than the polish on your shoes.

Con sus insultos quedó a la altura del betún.
His insults made him look really bad.

Knowledge, intelligence, ignorance and understanding

haberse caído del guindo

"to have fallen out of the cherry tree"
= to have been born yesterday

¿No te pensarás que me he caído del guindo?
Do you think I was born yesterday?

ser más listo que Lepe

"to be smarter than Lepe"
= to be pretty smart

The Lepe in question was a seventeenth-century Spanish bishop, famed for his vast learning and intelligence – the Einstein of his day. Remember that with **ser**, **listo** means *smart*, but with **estar** it means *ready*.

Ese primo tuyo es más listo que Lepe.
That cousin of yours is pretty smart.

saber la biblia en verso

"to know the bible in verse"
= to know absolutely everything

A very untalented nineteenth-century Spanish writer versified part of the Bible, which gave rise to this phrase, often with a suggestion of something long and tedious.

Pregúntale cualquier cosa, se sabe la biblia en verso.
Ask him anything, he knows absolutely everything.

ser una lanza

> *"to be a lance"*
> = to be really on the ball

Puede que parezca tonto, pero ese chico es una lanza.
He may seem stupid but that boy is really on the ball.

conocer algo como la palma de la mano

> *"to know something like the palm of your hand"*
> = to know something like the back of your hand

This is another phrase where Spanish and English are similar, yet subtly different.

Se conoce la ciudad como la palma de la mano.
He knows the city like the back of his hand.

no saber ni jota de algo

"not to know even letter j about something"
= not to know the first thing about something

Another phrase to convey the same idea is **no saber ni papa de algo** (*not to know even a potato about something*).

No sabe ni jota de informática.
He doesn't know the first thing about IT.

oír campanas y no saber de dónde vienen

"to hear bells and not know where they're coming from"
= not to have a clue

In this phrase, and the next, notice how the question words **dónde** and **qué** have accents.

Ese ha oído campanas y no sabe de dónde vienen.
He doesn't have a clue.

ser un águila

"to be an eagle"
= to be very sharp

This refers to being sharp in general, not merely to being eagle-eyed.

Es un águila y ve las oportunidades donde los demás no vemos nada.
He's very sharp, and he sees opportunities where the rest of us don't see anything.

no saber de qué va la fiesta

> *"not to know what the party's about"*
> = not to have a clue

Si quieres que te diga la verdad, no sé de qué va la fiesta.
To tell you the truth, I haven't got a clue.

no saber de la misa la media

> *"not to know half the mass"*
> = not to have a clue

You can also say **no saber de la misa la mitad.**

Habla mucho pero no sabe de la misa la media.
He talks a lot but he hasn't got a clue.

tomar el rábano por las hojas

"to take hold of the radish by the leaves"
= to get the wrong end of the stick

If you start to eat a radish from the leaves, you obviously don't know how to eat radishes – or, it is implied, much else.

Estás tomando el rábano por las hojas. ¿Por qué no me escuchas?
You are getting the wrong end of the stick.
Why don't you listen to me?

lo saben hasta las piedras

"even stones know that"
= it's common knowledge
= everyone knows that

Están saliendo juntos, lo saben hasta las piedras.
They're going out together, everyone knows that.

me suena a chino

"it sounds like Chinese to me"
= it's all Greek to me

Esas instrucciones me suenan a chino.
Those instructions are all Greek to me.

Looks, appearance, beauty and vanity

estar hecho un espárrago

"to be an asparagus"

= to be as thin as a rake

English uses a gardening image, and Spanish uses a food analogy. Another phrase used to describe somebody thin is **estar como un fideo** (*to be as thin as a spaghetti*).

Debería comer más, está hecho un espárrago.

He should eat more, he's as thin as a rake.

el hábito no hace al monje

"the habit doesn't make the monk"
= don't judge by appearances
= don't judge a book by its cover

Puede que no parezca un profesional, pero el hábito no hace al monje.
He may not look like a professional, but you shouldn't judge by appearances.

estar hecho un Adán

"to be like Adam"
= to look a sight
= to look like something the cat dragged in

Estás hecho un Adán, ¿no pensarás ir a la fiesta así?
You look a sight. You're not thinking of going to the party like that, are you?

tener ángel

"to have angel"
= to have charm
= to be very charming

You can apply this expression to somebody who has great charm, even if they are not good-looking. The idea is an angel must be looking after them.

Esa chica tiene ángel.
That girl is very charming.

más feo que Picio

"uglier than Picio"
= as ugly as sin

Picio, poor chap, appears to have been a real person in nineteenth-century Spain. Another expression is **feo como un grajo** (*as ugly as a rook*).

Su novio es más feo que Picio.
Her boyfriend is as ugly as sin.

no necesitar abuela

"not to need a grandmother"
= to be full of yourself
= to blow your own trumpet

Grandparents dote on their grandchildren, and praise whatever they do. So if somebody doesn't need a grandmother to praise them, it's because they do it themselves!

Ese no necesita abuela, siempre elogiándose.
He is so full of himself he doesn't need anyone else to praise him.

tener la cabeza como una bola de billar

"to have your head like a billiard ball"

= to be as bald as a coot

What could be more lacking in hair than a billiard ball?

Lo reconocerás fácilmente porque tiene la cabeza como una bola de billar. You'll easily recognize him because he's as bald as a coot.

un hombre de pelo en pecho

"*a man with hair on his chest*"
= a real man

Dice que quiere un hombre de pelo en pecho.
She says she wants a real man.

chupar cámara

"to suck the camera"

= to get a lot of media attention

This sarcastic phrase refers to politicians, celebs and the like – you know who they are – who love being filmed and photographed at every possible opportunity.

Es uno de esos políticos a los que les gusta chupar cámara.
He's one of those politicians who like to get a lot of media attention.

Madness, foolishness and stupidity

estar más loco que una cabra

"to be madder than a goat"
= to be as mad as a hatter

Goats' behaviour is somewhat unpredictable, hence the image.

Mi profesor de física está más loco que una cabra.
My physics teacher is as mad as a hatter.

estar mal de la azotea

> *"to have a problem on your roof terrace"*
> = to be off your head
> = to have bats in the belfry

Azoteas are the tiled terraces that you might see on traditional houses with flat roofs. As in English, this phrase uses the highest point of a building as a metaphor for the head.

Tú estás mal de la azotea, ¿cómo se te ocurre decir esa tontería?
You're off your head. How can you say such rubbish?

estar como una regadera

> *"to be like a watering can"*
> = to have a screw loose

What's the connection? The idea is that the rose on the spout of a watering can has lots of little holes in it, as does the head, figuratively speaking, of the person you're referring to.

Mi tío está como una regadera.
My uncle has a screw loose.

estar loco de atar

"to be mad enough to tie up"
= to be stark raving mad
= to be off your head

¿Estás loco de atar?, ¿quieres que nos castiguen?
Are you off your head? Do you want them to punish us?

perder la chaveta

"to lose your pin"
= to go off your head
= to really flip

Intenté tranquilizarle pero perdió la chaveta.
I tried to calm him down, but he really flipped.

estar en la luna de Valencia

> "to be in the Valencia moon"
> = to be daydreaming

Valencia is an important port city in Spain, and some believe that the origin of this expression dates from medieval times when the walls of the city were closed at night, leaving those outside with only the moon as shelter.

Estás en la luna de Valencia, ¿o qué?
Are you daydreaming or what?

estar en Babia

> "to be in Babia"
> = to be on another planet

What and where is Babia? One suggestion is that it was where a medieval Spanish king went to to get away from the Court. Over time, the phrase came to mean mental rather than physical absence.

Parece que estés en Babia, ¿te has enterado de lo que he dicho?
You seem to be on another planet. Did you take in what I said?

tener pájaros en la cabeza

"to have birds in your head"
= to be empty-headed
= to be completely dopey

No le hagas mucho caso, tiene pájaros en la cabeza.
Don't take any notice of him, he's completely dopey.

más bruto que un arado

> *"more stupid than a plough"*
> = as dumb as an ox

No dejes que toque el ordenador, es más bruto que un arado.
Don't let him touch the computer, he's as dumb as an ox.

ser un animal de bellota

> *"to be an animal of acorns"*
> = to be as thick as two short planks

The most highly-prized Spanish ham is **jamón de bellota** (*acorn ham*). It comes from pigs which are left to wander freely in oak forests to fatten up.

Eres un animal de bellota, te lo voy a explicar otra vez.
You're as thick as two short planks. Let me explain it to you again.

ser de pocas luces

"to have few lights"
= to be not very bright

No esperes mucho de ella, es de pocas luces.
Don't expect a lot of her, she's not very bright.

no tener dos dedos de frente

"not to have two fingers' width of forehead"
= to be as thick as two short planks

Parece que no tiene dos dedos de frente.
He seems to be as thick as two short planks.

Relationships, similarities and differences

son lobos de una camada

"they're wolves of one litter"
= they're birds of a feather

No te quejes de tus compañeros que sois todos lobos de una camada.
Don't complain about your classmates, you're all birds of a feather.

ni de aquí a Lima

"not from here to Lima"
= there's just no comparison
= not by a long chalk

The vast distance between Spain and Lima, the capital of Peru, emphasizes the difference between the things you're talking about.

Maradona no fue mejor que Pelé, ni de aquí a Lima.
Maradona wasn't better than Pelé – not by a long chalk.

no es santo de mi devoción

"he's not a saint of my devotion"
= he's not my cup of tea

People often have a saint that they're particularly devoted to.

Sabes perfectamente que tu hermano no es santo de mi devoción.
You know perfectly well that your brother's not my cup of tea.

ser uña y carne

"to be nail and flesh"
= to be inseparable
= to be as thick as thieves

Elsa y Clara son uña y carne.
Elsa and Clara are as thick as thieves.

cojean del mismo pie

"they limp with the same foot"
= they're two of a kind

Los dos cojean del mismo pie y no saben decir que no a una botella de vino.
They're two of a kind and they can't say no to a bottle of wine.

Dios los cría y ellos se juntan

"God brings them up and they get together"
= birds of a feather flock together

Todos sus amigos son también programadores: Dios los cría y ellos se juntan.
All his friends are programmers too – birds of a feather flock together.

no hay que confundir la gimnasia con la magnesia

"you mustn't confuse gymnastics and magnesium"
= let's not muddle up two totally different things
= let's not confuse matters

No hay que confundir la gimnasia con la magnesia, una cosa es ser franco, otra es ser grosero.
Let's not confuse matters. It's one thing to be frank, and another to be rude.

me cae gordísimo

"he falls on me very very fat"
= I can't stand him

The **ísimo** ending on an adjective means 'very, very': **Es altísimo** (He's very, very tall).

La nueva profesora de química me cae gordísima.
I can't stand the new chemistry teacher.

no se parecen ni en el blanco de los ojos

"they don't resemble each other even in the whites of their eyes"

= to be like chalk and cheese

Mis hermanas no se parecen ni en el blanco de los ojos.
My sisters are as different as chalk and cheese.

Problems, difficulties, the possible and the impossible

cuando las ranas críen pelo

"when frogs will grow hair"
= pigs might fly

Te dejaré el dinero cuando las ranas críen pelo.
Yeah, I'll lend you the money – and pigs might fly!

ahogarse en un vaso de agua

> *"to drown in a glass of water"*
> = to make a mountain out of a molehill

Mi madre es de las que se ahoga en un vaso de agua.
My mother's one of those people who make mountains out of molehills.

ir de Guatemala a Guatepeor

> *"to go from Guatebad to Guateworse"*
> = to jump out of the frying pan into the fire

This is a pun on the name of the Central American country. **Malo** means *bad*, and its comparative is **peor**, meaning *worse*.

Con este nuevo gobierno vamos de Guatemala a Guatepeor.
With this new government, we're jumping out of the frying pan into the fire.

estar entre la espada y la pared

"to be between the sword and the wall"
= to be between the devil and the deep blue sea

Estoy entre la espada y la pared, y sinceramente no sé qué hacer.
I'm caught between the devil and the deep blue sea, and frankly I don't know what to do.

no hay mal que por bien no venga

"there is no bad that doesn't turn out well"
= every cloud has a silver lining

Why the subjunctive **venga**? Because it follows **no hay**. You use the subjunctive to say that something doesn't exist, or isn't the case: **No tiene a nadie que le ayude** (*He doesn't have anybody to help him*).

No hay mal que por bien no venga: esa lluvia es una bendición para el campo.
Every cloud has a silver lining: that rain is a blessing for the countryside.

pedir peras al olmo

> *"to ask the elm tree for pears"*
> = to ask for the impossible

Here's another phrase with pears. What could be more impossible than expecting an elm tree to produce them?

Querer que Carlos saque buenas notas es pedir peras al olmo.
Wanting Carlos to get good marks is asking for the impossible.

a perro flaco todo son pulgas

> *"to a thin dog it's all fleas"*
> = it never rains but it pours

A perro flaco todo son pulgas: primero las piedras en el riñón y ahora el cáncer.
It never rains but it pours: first of all kidney stones, and now cancer.

meter palos en las ruedas

> *"to put sticks in the wheels"*
> = to throw a spanner in the works
> = to put a spoke in the wheels

El presidente pidió a la oposición que esta vez no metiera palos en las ruedas.
The president asked the opposition not to throw a spanner in the works this time.

es pan comido

> *"it's bread that's been eaten"*
> = it's a piece of cake

No te preocupes que esto es pan comido, te lo arreglo en cinco minutos.
Don't worry, this is a piece of cake. I can fix it for you in five minutes.

no todo el monte es orégano

> *"not all the hillside is oregano"*
> = life isn't a bed of roses

Oregano can grow wild on the hills, and makes good grazing for sheep and goats.

Cuando crezcas descubrirás que no todo el monte es orégano.
When you grow up, you'll find out that life isn't a bed of roses.

esto no tiene mucha ciencia

> *"this doesn't have a lot of science"*
> = there's nothing difficult about it

Lo voy a resolver rápidamente porque esto no tiene mucha ciencia.
It won't take me long to sort out because there's nothing difficult about it.

no lo voy a hacer ni loco

> *"I'm not going to do it even if mad"*
> = nothing in the world would make me do it

You use this phrase when there really is no way you'll do something.

No voy a pedirle perdón ni loco.
Nothing in the world would make me apologize to him.

parece mentira que ...

"it seems a lie that ..."
= I can't believe that ...
= It seems impossible that ...

⬤ You'll notice how you use the subjunctive after this phrase.

Parece mentira que tenga que repetir esto todos los dias.
I can't believe I have to say the same thing every day.

a buenas horas mangas verdes

"in good time green sleeves"
= it's too late now

⬤ You use this to criticize somebody who offers help, but turns up too late to be of any use. In the 15th century the rural police in Spain wore uniforms with green sleeves – and they were notorious for turning up too late, after the event.

A buenas horas mangas verdes, tu invitación ya no me sirve.
It's too late now, your invitation's no use to me anymore.

en dos patadas

> *"in two kicks"*
> = in a flash
> = in no time

Llegaré ahí en dos patadas.
I'll be there in no time.

Orders, obedience, control and equality

pagar el pato

"to pay for the duck"
= to carry the can

¿Por qué tengo que ser yo el que siempre pague el pato?
Why do I always have to be the one who carries the can?

tener la sartén por el mango

> *"to hold the frying pan by the handle"*
> = to call the shots
> = to be the boss

Aquí en casa la que tiene la sartén por el mango es ella.
She's the one who calls the shots at home.

cortar el bacalao

> *"to cut the bacalao"*
> = to be in charge
> = to call the shots

Bacalao is dried, salted cod, still used in some typical
Spanish dishes. Before refrigeration, fish was dried and
salted to preserve it, and the person entrusted with cutting
such a delicacy was clearly in charge.

Quiero hablar con el que realmente corta el bacalao aquí.
I want to speak to the person who's really in charge here.

tener a alguien más derecho que una vela

"to have somebody straighter than a sail"
= to have somebody under your thumb

Just like English, Spanish has many phrases deriving from its seafaring history.

El profesor de inglés los tiene más derechos que una vela.
The English teacher's really got them under his thumb.

pagar los platos rotos

"to pay for the broken plates"
= to carry the can

A phrase to be used when somebody takes the rap for something that is not their fault.

Esta vez va a ser mi hermana la que pague los platos rotos.
This time it's going to be my sister who carries the can.

cargar con el muerto

> *"to carry the dead man"*
> = to carry the can

In medieval Spain, if the body of someone who met a violent death was found, and the culprit was not discovered, the locals would have to pay a fine. To avoid this, they would carry the body and dump it within the boundaries of the next village or town.

Pueden buscar a otro porque no pienso cargar con el muerto.
They can look for somebody else because I have no intention of carrying the can.

tener a alguien metido en el bote

> *"to have somebody put in the jar"*
> = to have somebody eating out of your hand

Tengo a mi jefe metido en el bote.
I've got my boss eating out of my hand.

llevar la batuta

"to carry the baton"
= to be in charge

The baton here is a conductor's baton.

Yo soy el que llevo la batuta en la oficina.
I'm the one who's in charge in the office.

al pie de la letra

> *"to the foot of the letter"*
> = to the letter
> = exactly

Seguí las instrucciones al pie de la letra.
I followed the instructions to the letter.

bailar el agua a alguien

> *"to dance the water to somebody"*
> = to suck up to somebody

Siempre les ha bailado el agua a los jefes.
He's always sucked up to the bosses.

bailar al son que tocan

"to dance to the tune they're playing"
= to toe the line

Estamos acostumbrados a bailar al son que tocan.
We're used to toeing the line.

Work, achievement, effort and ambition

trabajar como un burro

"to work like a donkey"

= to work like a dog

= to work your socks off

Donkeys feature in many colourful phrases, such as this one.

Trabajé como un burro para entregar la redacción a tiempo.
I worked my socks off to hand in the essay on time.

tirar del carro

> *"to pull the cart"*
> = to do the donkey work

Siempre tiene que haber alguien que tire del carro.
There always has to be somebody to do the donkey work.

trabajar como una hormiga

> *"to work like an ant"*
> = to work very hard
> = to slog away

Acumuló una pequeña fortuna después de trabajar como una hormiga durante décadas.
She amassed a small fortune after working very hard for decades.

ganarse las lentejas

"to earn your lentils"

= to earn a living

= to earn a crust

A similar expression is **ganarse los garbanzos** (*to earn your chickpeas*).

Acepta cualquier tipo de trabajo porque, como todo el mundo, tiene que ganarse las lentejas.
He accepts any kind of work because, like everybody, he needs to earn a living.

un trabajo de chinos

"a job for Chinese people"
= a fiddly job

Chinese decorative goods – such as porcelain and lacquerware – were highly prized historically in Europe. This phrase refers to the patience needed to make these delicate, detailed and exquisite objects.

Montar la estantería fue un auténtico trabajo de chinos.
Putting up the bookcase was a really fiddly job.

unos cardan la lana y otros cobran la fama

"some card the wool and others gain the glory"
= some do all the work and others take all the credit

Carding wool involves cleaning and combing it to make it suitable for weaving: extremely hard, manual work, before machines were invented to do the job.

Todos sabemos de quién fue el mérito, pero unos cardan la lana y otros cobran la fama.
We all know who the credit belongs to, but some do all the work, and others take all the credit.

no se ganó Zamora en una hora

"Zamora was not won in an hour"
= Rome wasn't built in a day

You use this rhyming phrase to remind people that achieving something worthwhile takes time. The town of Zamora lies in the autonomous region of Castille and León, in northwest Spain, and was the site of an epic siege in the 11th Century.

Vamos con calma, que no se ganó Zamora en una hora.
Let's take things slowly. Rome wasn't built in a day.

quemarse las pestañas

"to singe your eyelashes"
= to burn the midnight oil

You can imagine studying by lamp – or candlelight, and being so near to them that you singe your eyelashes. The reflexive **quemarse** is used, as with so many actions referring to parts of the body.

Se ha quemado las pestañas durante un mes para preparar el examen.
He burnt the midnight oil for a month studying for the exam.

se le va la fuerza por la boca

> *"his strength goes out through his mouth"*
> = he's all talk and no action
> = he's all mouth and no trousers

Es muy bravucón pero se le va la fuerza por la boca.
He's full of bluster, but he's all talk and no action.

poner toda la carne en el asador

> *"to put all the meat on the barbecue"*
> = to pull out all the stops

If you put all your meat on the barbie at the same time, you're leaving nothing in reserve.

Vamos a tener que poner toda la carne en el asador si queremos derrotarlos.
We're going to have to pull out all the stops if we want to beat them.

rascarse la barriga

"to scratch your belly"
= to do damn all
= to sit on your backside

No te quedes ahí sentado rascándote la barriga y ven a ayudarme.
Don't just sit there on your backside: come and help me.

sacar fuerzas de flaqueza

> *"to drag strength out of weakness"*
> = to make a supreme effort

Tuve que sacar fuerzas de flaqueza para conseguir llegar a la cumbre.
I had to make a supreme effort to manage to get to the summit.

Change, continuity, risk and opportunity

ser un culo de mal asiento

"to be a backside that can't sit still"

= to have ants in your pants

¡Pero qué culo de mal asiento eres! ¿No te podrías quedar quieto un rato?

Have you got ants in your pants? Can't you sit still for a minute?

entre col y col, lechuga

> *"betweeen cabbage and cabbage, lettuce"*
> = variety is the spice of life
> = just for a change

Legend has it that a particular Spanish king used to eat cabbage salads in order to lose weight and sometimes lettuce would be added for a bit of variety in his diet!

Entre col y col, lechuga: vamos a hacer un inciso para hablar de arte.
Just for a change, we're going to digress and talk about art.

borrón y cuenta nueva

> *"crossing out and a new sum"*
> = let's make a fresh start

If you make a mistake while doing a sum, you cross it out and start again. This phrase suggests the same applies to life.

Le pides perdón y borrón y cuenta nueva.
You apologize to her and make a fresh start.

a otra cosa, mariposa

> *"to something else, butterfly"*
> = let's move on to something else

⬤ You use this phrase to emphasize that a particular topic or event is over. Its rhyme gives it a suitable finality.

Vamos a acabar de leer este capítulo, y a otra cosa, mariposa.
Let's finish reading this chapter, and then move on to something else.

cambiar el chip

> *"to change the chip"*
> = to change your attitude to something

⬤ With its reference to microchips, this phrase is clearly modern. The idea is that your mind is an electronic device, and by putting in a different chip you can change your outlook.

Ya es hora de que cambies el chip y te des cuenta de que estás en la universidad.
It's time to change your attitude and realize that you're at university.

la ocasión la pintan calva

"they depict opportunity as bald"
= you have to grab the opportunity

Ocasión can mean an opportunity as well as an occasion. The phrase relates to the image of opportunity as a goddess. She's bald because in Spanish you have to *seize opportunity by the hair* (**coger la ocasión por los pelos**).

Me presenté candidato de inmediato porque la ocasión la pintan calva.
I applied right away, because you have to grab the opportunity while it's there.

hay moros en la costa

"there are Moors on the coast"
= watch out

Much of the Spanish coast is within easy distance of North Africa, and historically Moorish pirates from there raided Spanish ports. This phrase is a warning that an adult or somebody in authority is around.

Esconde el cigarrillo que hay moros en la costa.
Watch out! Somebody's coming. Hide the cigarette.

no está el horno para bollos

"the oven isn't ready for buns"
= the time isn't right

Yo no discutiría el asunto con nuestros padres, no está el horno para bollos.
I wouldn't talk about it with mum and dad, the time isn't right.

Motion, travel, leaving and parting

en el quinto infierno

"in the fifth hell"
= at the back of beyond

This diabolical image has a colourful Latin American version: **donde el diablo perdió el poncho** (*where the Devil lost his poncho*).

Vive en el quinto infierno.
He lives at the back of beyond.

a toda mecha

"at full fuse"
= like greased lightning

The fuse here must be the fuse on an old-fashioned cannon.

Subió las escaleras a toda mecha.
She went up the stairs like greased lightning.

irse pitando

"to go off whistling"
= to be off like a shot
= to rush off

This phrase refers to steam trains blowing their whistles as they leave the station.

Me voy pitando que se me hace tarde.
I'm going to be late; I must rush off.

despedirse a la francesa

"to say goodbye in the French way"
= to leave without saying goodbye

France once set the trend in etiquette for the rest of Europe. Supposedly, in the 17th century, it was de rigueur not to bid farewell when leaving upper-crust gatherings in Paris. Hence the expression.

Una vez más se despidieron a la francesa.
Yet again they left without saying goodbye.

andando, que es gerundio

"going, which is gerund"
= we'd better get a move on

You use this phrase to hurry along somebody who is dawdling. The gerund in Spanish is the form of the verb ending in *-ndo*.

¡Ya son las once! ¡Andando, que es gerundio!
It's eleven already! We'd better get a move on!

salir como alma que lleva el diablo

"to leave like a soul that the Devil is carrying"
= to leave like a bat out of hell

The Devil is always in a hurry, it seems, to rush your soul off to Hell.

Cuando vio entrar a su ex, salió como alma que lleva el diablo.
When he saw his ex come in, he left like a bat out of hell.

ahuecar el ala

"to hollow the wing"
= to beat it

Será mejor que ahuequemos el ala.
We'd better beat it.

hacer dedo

"to do thumb"
= to hitch-hike

Pensábamos hacer dedo hasta la playa.
We were thinking of hitching to the beach.

cortarse la coleta

"to cut off your pigtail"
= to quit
= to retire

The pigtail is a bullfighting reference. At their last bullfight before retiring, bullfighters ceremonially cut of the false pigtail attached to their hat.

Dijo que no pensaba cortarse la coleta todavía.
He said he wasn't thinking of retiring yet.

Chance, surprise and the unexpected

se le pusieron los ojos como platos

"her/his eyes became like plates"
= her/his eyes nearly fell out of their sockets

A phrase that forcefully conveys the look on the face of somebody who is very surprised.

Cuando vio el anillo, se le pusieron los ojos como platos.
When she saw the ring, her eyes nearly fell out of their sockets.

se me puso la piel de gallina

"I got chicken skin"
= I got goose pimples

A similar image to English, but with a different bird.

Se nos puso la piel de gallina cuando escuchamos el alarido.
We got goose pimples when we heard the scream.

por si las moscas

"just in case the flies"
= just in case
= just to be on the safe side

Yo llamaría antes, por si las moscas.
I'd call first, just to be on the safe side.

¿qué aires te traen por aquí?

"what breezes bring you here?"

= what a surprise to see you here!

= what brings you here?

¡Pero si es Alberto! ¿Qué aires te traen por aquí?
Well, if it isn't Alberto! What brings you here?

quedarse de piedra

"to turn to stone"

= to be stunned

Cuando me contó que se había divorciado, me quedé de piedra.
When he told me he'd got divorced, I was stunned.

blanco como la cera

"as white as wax"

= as white as a sheet

To convey how the colour drains from your face through shock and surprise, Spanish also refers to walls and paper: **blanco como la pared** (*white like the wall*), **blanco como el papel** (*white like paper*).

¿Qué te ha pasado? ¡Estás blanca como la cera!
What's happened to you? You're as white as a sheet!

como llovido del cielo

"as if rained from the sky"

= heaven-sent

= like a godsend

Su ayuda nos vino como llovida del cielo.
Her help was a godsend for us.

quedarse bizco

"to turn cross-eyed"
= to be gobsmacked

Quedarse, as in this phrase and the next, is sometimes used to describe changes caused by external circumstances: **Se quedó viuda** *(She was widowed)*.

Me quedé bizco viéndola cocinar.
I was gobsmacked when I watched her cook.

Eating, drinking, drunkenness and excess

comer a dos carrillos

"to eat with two cheeks"

= to stuff your face

Estaban sentados a la mesa comiendo a dos carrillos.
They were sitting at the table stuffing their faces.

tener buen diente

> *"to have a good tooth"*
> = to be a hearty eater
> = to have a healthy appetite

He preparado bastante comida porque los invitados tienen buen diente.
I've made quite a lot of food because the guests have healthy appetites.

esto sabe a demonios

> *"this tastes of devils"*
> = this tastes really awful

Few, if any, living people know what devils taste like, but it's a fair bet they aren't exactly delicious.

Este filete sabe a demonios.
This steak tastes really awful.

vivir a cuerpo de rey

"to live like the body of a king"
= to live like a king

The Spanish phrase emphasizes the bodily indulgence and comforts of being a king.

Vive a cuerpo de rey en casa de sus padres.
He lives like a king at his parents'.

ponerse morado

"to go purple"
= to stuff yourself

Nos pusimos morados de comer cerezas.
We stuffed ourselves with cherries.

beber como una esponja

"to drink like a sponge"
= to drink like a fish

An alternative to this is **beber como un cosaco** (*to drink like a Cossack*).

Tu tío bebe como una esponja.
Your uncle drinks like a fish.

borracho como una cuba

"as drunk as a wine barrel"
= completely plastered
= as drunk as a skunk

You can also simply say **como una cuba**.

El conductor que provocó el accidente estaba borracho como una cuba.
The driver who caused the accident was completely plastered.

empinar el codo

"to bend your elbow"

= to booze

Todos conocen su afición a empinar el codo.
Everybody knows he's fond of boozing.

en cantidades industriales

> *"in industrial quantities"*
> = by the bucketload

Había comida y bebida en cantidades industriales.
There was food and drink by the bucketload.

Directness, decisiveness and expressing opinions

consultarlo con la almohada

"*to consult your pillow about it*"
= to sleep on it

Voy a consultarlo con la almohada y mañana te doy una respuesta.
I'm going to sleep on it, and I'll give you an answer tomorrow.

echar sapos y culebras por la boca

"to throw toads and snakes out of your mouth"
= to turn the air blue
= to swear your head off
= to use very strong language

Cuando entramos en la tienda, había un cliente echando sapos y culebras por la boca.
When we went into the shop, there was a customer turning the air blue.

al pan pan, y al vino vino

"call bread bread and wine wine"
= I believe in calling a spade a spade
= I'm not going to mince my words

The Spanish staples of bread and wine provide the image for plain speaking.

Al pan pan, y al vino vino: es un auténtico canalla.
I'm not going to mince my words, he's a real swine.

no tener pelos en la lengua

"not to have hairs on your tongue"

= not to mince your words

If you had hairs on your tongue, it would be hard to say what you really mean.

No tiene pelos en la lengua y siempre dice lo que piensa.
He doesn't mince his words and he always says what he thinks.

hablar a calzón quitado

"to talk with your underpants off"

= to talk openly

= to talk with no holds barred

Los dos presidentes hablaron a calzón quitado sin la presencia de sus asistentes.
The two presidents talked with no holds barred in the absence of their assistants.

¿a ti quién te ha dado vela en este entierro?

"who gave you a candle at this funeral?"
= what business is it of yours?

¿A ti quién te ha dado vela en este entierro? Esta discusión no tiene nada que ver contigo.
What business is it of yours? This argument has nothing to do with you.

me salió del alma

"it came out from my soul"
= it just came out
= I said it without thinking

Después me arrepentí, pero el insulto me salió del alma.
I regretted it afterwards, but the insult just came out.

mentar la soga en casa del ahorcado

> *"to mention the rope in the house of the hanged man"*
> = to put your foot in it

This proverb was famously used by Don Quijote.

Ni se te ocurra preguntar por su ex marido, no vayas a mentar la soga en casa del ahorcado.
Don't even think about asking about her ex-husband. That would be really putting your foot in it!

nadar entre dos aguas

> *"to swim between two waters"*
> = to sit on the fence

Siempre ha sido de los que nadan entre dos aguas sin comprometerse con nadie.
He's always been one of those people who sit on the fence without committing to anybody.

no saber a qué carta quedarse

"not to know which card to stay with"
= not to know which one to run with

An image from card games where you have to decide which cards to hang on to, and which to take from the pack.

Las dos propuestas me parecen excelentes y no sé a qué carta quedarme.
The two proposals look excellent to me, and I don't know which one to run with.

se cae por su propio peso

"it falls from its own weight"
= it goes without saying

The image in this rather formal phrase suggests a ripe fruit ready to drop.

Se cae por su propio peso que ahora deberíamos ayudarle nosotros.
It goes without saying that we should help him now.

¡para el carro!

"stop the cart!"

= hang on!

= hold your horses!

¡Para el carro! ¿De dónde va a salir el dinero para el viaje?
Hold your horses! Where's the money for the trip going to come from?

hablar del sexo de los ángeles

"to talk about the sex of the angels"
= to indulge in pointless discussion

This phrase clearly comes from the same stable of medieval theological navel-gazing that gave English the similar phrase for pointless discussion: *How many angels can dance on the head of a pin?*

Me parece que estamos hablando del sexo de los ángeles.
I think this discussion is pointless.

Money, debt, wealth and poverty

atan los perros con longaniza

"they tie up dogs with sausages"
= the streets are paved with gold

You'd have to be very rich to tie up dogs with sausages, as they'd only eat them. This phrase goes back to the 18th century, to a rich man's maid who really did tie up a dog with a string of sausages.

Hay gente que se piensa que en este país atan los perros con longaniza.
There are people who imagine that the streets are paved with gold in this country.

costar un ojo de la cara

"to cost an eye of your face"
= to cost an arm and a leg

Another way to emphasize how much something cost you is to refer to another part of your body: **Me costó un riñón** (*It cost me a kidney*).

El nuevo modelo cuesta un ojo de la cara.
The new model costs an arm and a leg.

criarse en buenos pañales

"to be raised in good nappies"
= to be born with a silver spoon in your mouth

Ese no sabe lo que es pasar hambre, se crió en buenos pañales.
He doesn't know what it is to be hungry. He was born with a silver spoon in his mouth.

el oro y el moro

"the gold and the Moor"
= the earth

Long ago some Spaniards held two Moorish noblemen to ransom. So greedy were the Spaniards that even after getting the money they kept their captives, and thus became a byword for a large amount of money.

Pedían el oro y el moro por un pisito minúsculo.
They were asking the earth for a tiny flat.

nadar en la abundancia

"to be swimming in abundance"
= to be rolling in it

En esta casa no se puede decir que nademos en la abundancia.
It couldn't be said we're rolling in it in this house.

rascarse el bolsillo

"*to scratch your pocket*"
= to put your hand in your pocket

Pedro fue el único que no quiso rascarse el bolsillo.
Pedro was the only one who refused to put his hand in his pocket.

ponerse las botas

"*to put on boots*"
= to be raking it in

Historically, only the rich could afford boots, hence the image of wealth this phrase suggests.

Abrieron un bar en un lugar muy turístico y se pusieron las botas.
They opened a bar in a tourist hotspot, and they raked it in.

tirar la casa por la ventana

"to throw the house through the window"

= to spare no expense

This curious phrase originates in the Spanish lottery, first set up in the 18th century. Winners threw their old furniture out of the window, to announce their new life was beginning. The custom survives at New Year in Naples, which was once under Spanish rule.

Era la boda de su hija y decidieron tirar la casa por la ventana.
It was their daughter's wedding and they decided to spare no expense.

comerse los codos de hambre

> *"to eat your elbows from hunger"*
> = not to have a penny to your name

Esos dos se comen los codos de hambre.
Those two don't have a penny to their name.

estar endeudado hasta las cejas

> *"to be up to your eyebrows in debt"*
> = to be up to your eyes in debt

No te puedo prestar nada porque estoy endeudado hasta las cejas.
I can't lend you anything because I'm up to my eyes in debt.

no tener más que el día y la noche

"to have only the day and the night"
= not to have two pennies to rub together

No nos pidáis nada, no tenemos más que el día y la noche.
Don't ask us for any anything, we haven't got two pennies to rub
together.

no tener un cuarto

"not to have a 'cuarto'"
= to be broke

Un cuarto was a coin of low value used long ago in Spain.
There are other variants of this expression, such as **no
tener un duro** (*not to have a five-peseta coin*), which is still used
despite the **peseta** no longer being in circulation, and **no
tener un céntimo** (*not to have a cent*).

¿Me podrías invitar? No tengo un cuarto.
Could you treat me? I'm broke.

Language, speech, silence and conversation

coserse la boca

"to sew up your mouth"
= to keep your lips sealed

Y será mejor que te cosas la boca.
You'd best keep your lips sealed.

hablar por los codos

"to talk through your elbows"
= to talk nineteen to the dozen

Ten cuidado con él porque habla por los codos.
Careful with him because he talks nineteen to the dozen.

enrollarse como una persiana

"to roll up like a blind"
= to go on and on

Me da miedo hablar con él porque siempre se enrolla como una persiana.
I'm wary of talking to him because he always goes on and on.

hablar en cristiano

"to speak in Christian"
= to speak in plain Spanish

At one time much of Spain was ruled by Moorish Arabs, and there was also a large Jewish community. Christian Spanish-speakers equated their own language with Christianity, as opposed to what the Arabs or Sephardic Jews spoke.

A mí háblame en cristiano, que no entiendo nada de lo que dices.
Talk to me in plain English, I can't understand a word of what you're saying.

no decir chus ni mus

"to say neither chus nor mus"
= not to say a word

Chus doesn't mean anything on its own outside this phrase. There is a card game called **mus**, but the use of the word here is probably to create a rhyme. You often hear a less colourful version of this expression: **no decir ni mu.**

Intenté sonsacarle lo que sabía pero no dijo ni chus ni mus.
I tried to worm out of him what he knew, but he didn't say a word.

no despegar los labios

> *"not to unstick your lips"*
> = not to utter a single word

No despegó los labios durante toda la reunión.
He didn't utter a single word the whole meeting.

seré una tumba

> *"I'll be a tomb"*
> = I won't breathe a word

No te preocupes, seré una tumba.
Don't worry, I won't breathe a word.

meter la cuchara

"to put in your spoon"
= to butt in
= to stick your oar in

People used to eat from a communal stewpot by dipping their spoons into it. From that comes the idea of sticking your oar into a conversation.

Siempre tienes que meter la cuchara.
You always have to stick your oar in.

no decir esta boca es mía

"not to say this mouth is mine"
= not to say a word

Si me preguntan, no pienso decir esta boca es mía.
If they ask me, I don't intend to say a word.

Youth, experience, age and death

estar todavía en pañales

"to be still in nappies"
= to be wet behind the ears

Es inteligente, pero todavía está en pañales.
She's bright, but she's still a bit wet behind the ears.

estar en la edad del pavo

"to be at the age of the turkey"
= to be at that difficult age

No le hagas mucho caso porque está en la edad del pavo.
Don't take any notice of her, she's at that awkward age.

peinar canas

"to comb grey hair"
= to be getting on

Spanish expresses the concept of *grey hair* with the plural word **las canas**.

Lo intenta ocultar pero ya peina canas.
He tries to hide it but he's getting on a bit.

criar gusanos

> *"to grow worms"*
> = to be pushing up daisies

El dictador cría gusanos en este cementerio.
The dictator is pushing up daisies in this cemetery.

estirar la pata

> "*to stretch your leg*"
> = to kick the bucket

Hace ahora un año que estiró la pata.
It's a year now since he kicked the bucket.

a la vejez viruelas

> "*to old age, smallpox*"
> = fancy that happening at his/her age

You use this phrase to show your surprise when somebody of a certain age does the unexpected.

Todos los fines de semana se va a subir montañas.
–¡A la vejez, viruelas!
Every weekend he heads off to go and climb mountains. – Fancy that, at his age!

ha llovido mucho desde entonces

"it's rained a lot since then"
= a lot of water has flowed under the bridge since then

En aquella época éramos muy amigos, pero ha llovido mucho desde entonces.
We were great friends in those days, but a lot of water has flowed under the bridge since then.

Index

Index

Uu

Vv

Zz

Have you seen our full Spanish range?
Pick a title to fit your learning style.

Dictionary
£8.99

Grammar
£6.99

Verbs
£6.99

Collins Easy Learning Series

The bestselling language resources, perfect if you're learning Spanish for the first time or brushing up on rusty skills.

Words
£6.99

Complete 3-in-1 volume
£10.99

Conversation
£6.99

Collins Easy Learning Audio Courses

This exciting course allows learners to absorb the basics at home or on the move, without the need for thick textbooks and complex grammar.

£9.99